MANHATTAN DAWN AND DUSK

MANHATTAN
DAWN
AND
DUSK
JON ORTNER

PREFACE BY
JOHN V. LINDSAY

INTRODUCTION BY
BRUCE KLUGER

STEWART, TABORI & CHANG

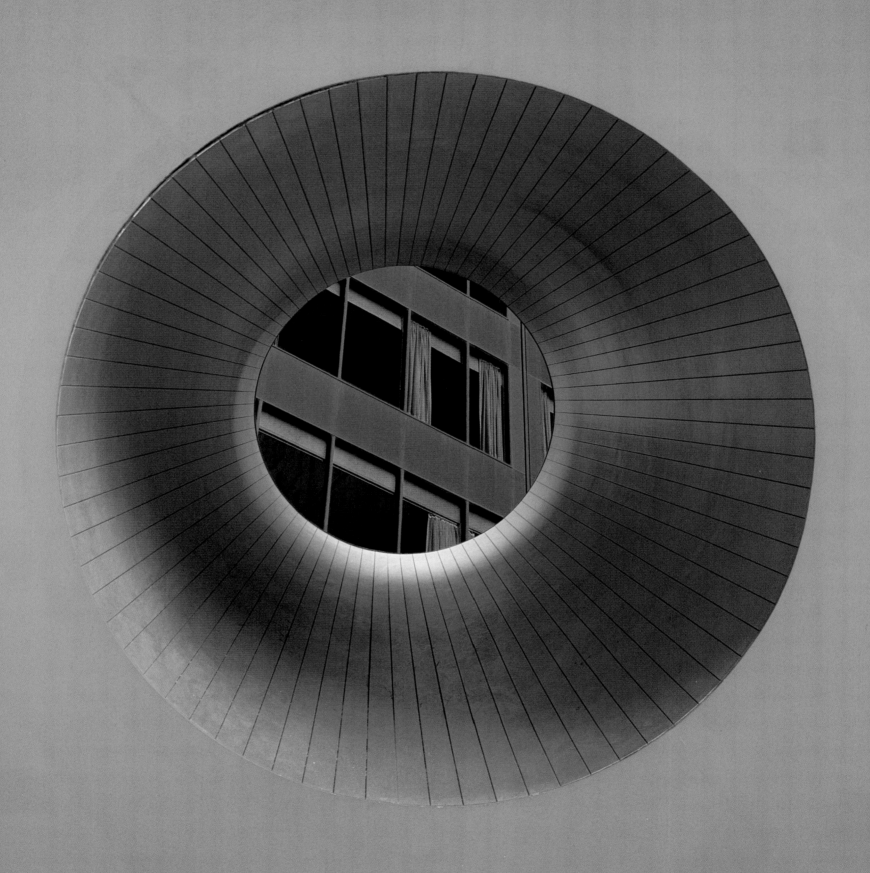

TO MY PARENTS
ANNE AND ARCHIE ORTNER

CONTENTS

ACKNOWLEDGMENTS

Photographs appearing in this book were created with the following equipment:

Nikon F3 and N90 cameras and Nikon lenses
Pentax 6x7 cameras and Pentax lenses
Linhof Technikardan 4x5 camera and Nikkor large-format lenses

SPECIAL THANKS TO:

Martha McGuire, Richard Ortner

John Cardasis, Mark Wayne, Ron Basile, Richard Berenholtz,
Brian Lawrence, Josh Kates, Neal Goldsmith, Larry Waxman

Jerry Grossman, Nikon Inc.,
Roberto Labog-Tanizaki, K & L Inc.
Tony and Sarah Stone, Tony Stone Images
Bob Gough, Director of Bridges for the N. Y. C. Department of Transportation
Kathryn Diminnie, Helen Bennett, and Nick Koutoufas of the N. Y. C. Convention & Visitors Bureau
N. Y. C. Mayor's Office of Film
Larry Winderbaum Inc., Chris Layton, Impact East
R. B. R. Color Labs, N. Y. C.

STEWART, TABORI & CHANG
Lena Tabori, Nai Chang, and all the talented staff at S. T. C.

FOREWORD

BY JON ORTNER

Stand with me at 5AM on the banks of the East River. Ignore the wind, ignore the cold. We are facing the massive, black wall of the Manhattan skyline dimly silhouetted against the night sky. Behind us, the eastern horizon begins to lighten, producing the first blush of color upon a multitude of windows. In the next ten minutes, as the dawn begins to unfold, the light will change a thousand times, but only a small number of fleeting images will capture the sky, cityscape, and reflection in perfect balance.

Now stand with me at Annapurna base camp in Nepal. Ignore the wind, ignore the cold—if you can! We are facing one of the largest ice walls in the Himalaya. Just before the sun appears on the horizon, its rays are deflected through the atmosphere, causing the peaks before us to reflect a pre-dawn spectrum of colors known as "alpenglow." As the sunlight sweeps across its face, the snow-covered precipice first turns powder blue, then pink, and finally, a blazing fiery orange.

These two scenes, half a world apart, may at first seem to be opposite extremes. Manhattan teems with human life and epitomizes the environment which man has built for himself, while Annapurna's crystalline slopes are sculpted by irresistible forces of nature. Yet underlying their inherent differences is a striking similarity of scale and grandeur. Even the vocabularies of the mountaineer and the architect overlap; both refer to spires, pinnacles, towers, buttresses, and columns. This vital link—nature's influence on mankind's architectural expression—goes back to the earliest civilizations.

Ancient people worshiped the highest mountain peaks as being the celestial homes of the gods. As Neolithic civilizations evolved, they worshiped natural formations and created temples that mimicked geometric shapes such as pyramids, dolmans, and obelisks. It is not a coincidence that today's modern skyscrapers also pay homage to these archetypal shapes.

The faceted surfaces of modern buildings can be compared to those of mountains, and even further, to diamonds, rubies, and emeralds. Crystals and gems have always been strong totem objects. Produced from the depths of Mother Earth, their color and light-capturing ability is a metaphor for mankind's highest aspirations (Light=God=Enlightenment). The glass and steel skyline of Manhattan, also crystalline, reflects the sun and all its colors as if the skyscrapers have grown from a matrix of bedrock.

In twenty years of traveling back and forth between New York and the Himalaya, these similarities have become striking and inescapable to me. I believe Manhattan is to cities what the Himalaya is to mountains.

◆ ◆ ◆

Some people collect antiques. I collect light. Film has a memory which stores the effects of light, something the eye cannot do. Subtle colors, invisible to the eye, can be intensified by film which records the quality and magnitude of light as it changes with the passage of time. Since the camera does not record what the mind sees, the photographer must develop the ability to penetrate beneath the surface with his vision to illustrate the inner character, or soul, of the chosen subject.

The challenges of photography in New York City are in some ways no less than those of the Himalaya. Finding the right vantage point is the central problem to be solved. The rest is a balance of persistence and technique. In both cases, the effort of climbing to the tops of bridges or negotiating an icy mountain pass can culminate in a magical synchronicity of weather, light, and position.

Just as a photojournalist seeks the "decisive moment," so are anomalous weather and atmospheric conditions the gesture and expression of a landscape photographer. Predicting storms, timing photo sessions to synchronize with moon phases, waiting for clouds to break during an overcast dawn—these are the elements common to the quest in both locations. Ansel Adams defined landscape photography as "the supreme test of the photographer—and often the supreme disappointment."

And just as titanic forces of plate tectonics have raised the highest mountain ranges in the world, so have the pressures of land restriction and population increase created today's Manhattan, the most dense concentration of massive buildings on the planet. The race for the tallest building is symbolic of man's unfailing optimism, and the skylines of our modern cities are temples to global commerce and technological achievement.

This is the vision of Manhattan that I want to share—a city painted with the rich colors of living, ever-changing light, a man-made mountain range where every detail speaks of the people who built it. We are all surrounded by the stunning visual landscape of the city, and with the right combinations of passion and patience, we can all experience the extraordinary beauty of Manhattan Dawn and Dusk.

PREFACE

BY JOHN V. LINDSAY

New York is a city of aspiration. Here, the soaring buildings and great bridges rise like cathedrals to vaulting ambition. How fitting then that Jon Ortner set out to capture the city at dawn and at dusk; for it is during these hours of anticipation that the city unfurls its limitless promises for the day and night ahead.

This glorious book begins, quite rightly, at the basin of New York harbor where Bartholdi's Statue of Liberty has welcomed generation after generation of immigrants to our shores. Though the currents of the East and Hudson rivers run treacherously swift, Lady Liberty seems to assure newcomers that the city's opportunities outweigh its risks.

From the Statue of Liberty's Centennial birthday celebration, illuminated by chrysanthemum fireworks, this volume proceeds, appropriately, to New York's financial district, awash with early morning sunlight. By evening, a trillion dollars' worth of transactions will have taken place within those few square blocks. No economy on earth will be left untouched by this commerce. Every day, the pulse of New York is felt all across the planet.

Lower Manhattan is also the seat of municipal government where, for eight years, it was my privilege to serve as mayor. No one has more information about the city at any given moment than the mayor. And throughout my years of service to the city, I was continually astonished at the city's infinite capacity to accommodate change. Even today, I marvel at the ability of this incredibly diverse, striving population to live in relative harmony and decency.

Moving north, we come upon SoHo. Since the early 1970s, the cast iron buildings in this former manufacturing district have been converted into artists' lofts, art galleries, restaurants and shops of all kinds. Here we see the city's protean quality; a neighborhood that shed an outmoded character to achieve a new purpose and identity. Transformed into this new incarnation, SoHo is a place whose art, design and cuisine influence styles all over the world.

Throughout the city, neighborhoods are defined in smaller, less obvious but no less meaningful ways. For example, a brilliant collage of fire escapes captures the quintessential feeling of Little Italy, one of New York's many transplanted corners of the Old World. George Gershwin, whose music captured the mythical yearnings and exaltations of the city, once said that he composed for young girls who pass hot summer nights sitting on such outdoor staircases, dreaming of love. Indeed, in New York City aspiration takes many forms.

Farther north, behold midtown Manhattan from the breathtaking vantage point atop the Empire State Building. Housed on this small patch of earth is every form of enterprise in every conceivable industry from law, fashion, advertising, manufacturing, computer technology, television production, publishing and recording to the English-speaking world's largest theater district. Also on this plot of land is the closest thing we have to a world government—the United Nations—making midtown Manhattan a place where international crises are occasionally resolved. Goods and services of all kinds are launched on their voyage across the globe through marketing plans hatched in this neighborhood. And products of the imagination that shape behavior and fantasy in every corner of the world originate here, too. Perhaps no where else on earth does so much that affects so many take place in such a small area. I often think that it's this incredible concentration of activity that makes New Yorkers walk tall, think fast and plan expansively. No wonder the city's atmosphere provokes accomplishment and inspires excellence.

For repose, we take in Central Park, an oasis of towering trees, green grass, flowers and refreshing quiet. Throughout the city's history, urban patriots have insisted on protecting and refining this exquisite place. As mayor, I did my part by closing Central Park and the city's other major parks to automobile traffic on weekends. A generation later, that ban is still in place, drawing people to these plush meadows and woodlands to cycle, hike, play ball and savor nature.

It is deeply pleasurable to gaze at Central Park's Belvedere Castle blanketed with snow and the tulips blooming on Park Avenue's median in spring. The city's elegance, romance, beauty and culture are to be found both in and around the Park. The distinguished apartment houses of Fifth, Madison and Park avenues and Central Park West, and the brownstones and other townhouses on their tree-lined side streets, have a grandeur and grace to rival Paris' finest *arrondissements*, London's Belgravia or Rome's *parioli* district. It is no exaggeration to add that in this part of town are some of the world's most precious museums—the Metropolitan, the Whitney, the Guggenheim, the Museum of Natural History, the Hayden Planetarium, and many others too numerous to list. Many of our indispensable universities and medical centers are also located nearby. These treasure troves of human achievement are monuments to New York's leadership in the arts and sciences.

Not far from the Park's southwestern gateway is Lincoln Center for the Performing Arts, the largest theatrical complex of its kind anywhere. After my career as a member of Congress and mayor, I served as chairman of the Lincoln Center Theater. Guiding that remarkable institution back to its current position as a showcase for some of the nation's best non-profit dramatic productions has truly been one of the major satisfactions in my career.

As these dazzling photographs demonstrate, Manhattan is the most magnificent man-made stage ever lit by the traveling sun. These scenes of unique urban splendor never fail to remind me of the young man or woman on a subway journey somewhere between home, school and a part-time job, fighting off distraction and fatigue while studying for an examination. That sort of determination and discipline, reflected in the great buildings and structures portrayed in this book, is the foundation of New York's finest achievements.

New York is a city of aspiration because it is a city of infinite possibilities. As mayor, I worked to make government a participant in the process of forging a cityscape that both elicits and expresses the best energies of our people. I cherish the architecture and urban design presented in this wonderful volume because they seem to bring within reach the chances for a fuller life.

Look at New York again in these pages and let the best of the city speak to the best in you.

John V. Lindsay, born in 1921, was a member of Congress from 1959-1966 and served as mayor of New York City from 1966-1973. He is currently a contributing editor for New York's public broadcasting station WNET Channel 13.

INTRODUCTION

Although I've lived in Manhattan just eighteen years, I feel uniquely qualified to write the introduction to *Manhattan Dawn and Dusk*, Jon Ortner's magnificent journey through the world's most mesmerizing, most photogenic city. The reason is simple: In all these years, my two most vivid memories of Manhattan are ones that occurred at, not coincidentally, sunup and sundown, those fleeting, ephemeral moments Ortner was wise—and talented—enough to have chosen as background music for the stunning photographic symphony you're about to enjoy.

The sunrise moment I experienced was not typical of the kind of dawns most folks choose to log into their memory banks—it included no waterfront scenery, no mountain-framed skyline, indeed, not even a sun. Instead, it took place at 5:30 AM in Manhattan's fashion district, the slate-gray, highrise-pocked strip of avenues that crisscross the city's midsection, just a shout from Macy's and Penn Station. I was an actor and on my way to shooting a commercial in which I'd been cast.

As I made my way to the location where the shoot would take place, I couldn't help but stop and notice how motionless Manhattan was at that dawn hour. And it wasn't just that the streets were bereft of people or cars; it was something more than that, almost as if the sensoral pause of the hour was actually designed to give the buildings and steel ramps and concrete blocks—even the puddles that necklaced the chunks of broken tarmac in the street—a quiet, secret moment to breathe and grow. I have never forgotten the solemnity of that morning, nor the scenery itself—and it is precisely this, the city's bone beneath the muscle, that Jon Ortner summons so successfully with his camera.

The ironic thing about the other Manhattan moment I remember most—the sundown—is that I wasn't even in New York at the time I witnessed it. I was living across the river in Hoboken, New Jersey, the tiny "miracle mile" of tenements, gardens and grocery stores that dot the west bank of the Hudson. On this particular fall evening I decided to take a dinner-time stroll through a small park that overlooked the river—an insignificant patch of green surrounded by a cast-iron fence.

As I stopped to take in the vista of the city I had moved hundreds of miles to be near, my breath was caught up short. There it was: Manhattan at dusk. The vista was endless—I could see from Battery Park in the south to Harlem way up north, the Chrysler and Empire State buildings piercing the still sky like runaway vines from an overgrown garden. Because a waterway separated me from the vibrant metropolis that is New York, the city's customary traffic horns and sirens were replaced by little more than the hum of the wind and the churning waves coming in off the river. The setting sun, meanwhile, had shrouded Manhattan in a brazen orange glow, freezing it in its own intensity and size. Years later I would remember this suspended moment when I saw, of all things, *Jurassic Park*, and learned how prehistoric tree sap formed a golden amber that preserved objects for an eternity. In this case, it was the sun that had caught the city at what appeared to be its dreamiest and most meditative moment.

So what do these two memories tell me about Manhattan and dawn and dusk? Does the sun, both setting and rising, pump a magical kind of blood through the rock and concrete capillaries of the island, giving it a split-second invincibility? Or is it just the opposite—does light from the heavens suspend the city in a wide-eyed stillness, just the way headlights briefly hypnotize a deer in an instant of breathless helplessness?

Clearly this was the mystery Jon Ortner hoped to unlock when he ventured high onto bridges and rooftops, and deep into fields and alleys, to photograph *Manhattan Dawn and Dusk*.

"This book looks the way it does not by chance," Jon Ortner says, kicking off a typical Ortnerian dissertation on photography, light and the endless joys of living on the giant rock-and-sand slab known as Manhattan. "I mean, take a look at the cover, for instance. I shot that image of the city with the sun setting behind me, its light reflecting in the glass windows over my shoulder. Now look carefully at the water. Did you know that the sun casts that kind of glow for, perhaps, only five or ten minutes a day? Not only that, but did you also know that the Hudson River looks the way it does there—completely still, yet always moving—maybe only once a year? I could go back to that location fifty or one hundred times—which, in fact, I probably did—without getting that kind of final image."

I have spoken to Jon Ortner about his past on a number of occasions, and am left feeling completely inspired by his life's work—a twenty-five-year mission that has taken him to the other side of the globe no less than ten times. Listening to him is like being drawn into a tornado. You are instantly overwhelmed by the sheer force of his passion, then whipped from story to story with head-spinning abandon, bombarded with tales that place you one moment at the tip-top of the Verrazano Narrows Bridge and the next on a Nepali river bank alongside a burning ghat.

But, in a way, Ortner's career seems almost destined to have happened. Originally a student of zoology and a naturalist, he found his way to his current livelihood via a confluence of diverse interests that awakened during his college years: photographing insects and flowers; working at the American Museum of Natural History; a burgeoning fascination with the Orient and India; and a seemingly innate curiosity about both spirituality and philosophy ("I am as enamored of Hinduism and Buddhism," he says, "as I am

with Einsteinian physics and how reality is structured."). Once he established himself as a professional photographer, he gained a reputation not only for his striking camera work, but for his intrepidness. To be sure, many of the stirring photos of Manhattan's skyline in this book were taken from the tops of bridges, and Ortner's retelling of those daring climbs are often as captivating as the images themselves.

"He's not just a traveler, and he's not just a photographer," says his former editor at *Geo*, Kevin Buckley, for whom Ortner photographed the wonders of Nepal. "He's an *explorer* in the true sense of the word. I had seen the Himalayas myself—but after I took a look at Jon's pictures, I felt I had really seen them."

Yet Ortner is the first to point out that photographing the majesty of the Himalayas is not so different from capturing the sun-painted vistas of Manhattan. In fact, he notes, the peaks, gorges and dramatic sweeps of the Himalayas are ironically reflected, almost identically, in the jagged rises and slopes of Manhattan. A true visualist, Ortner understands the complexities of that comparison: Unlike the panoramic canvases of the Nepali mountain ranges, New York is not a miracle of nature, nor is it a place where the man-made architecture is consistently perfect (or perfectly consistent). Yet both permit the photographer to step behind his camera and act as an interpreter of sorts, an artisan generously translating images we think we've seen a thousand times into a marvelous new language whose vocabulary is built on scraps and dabs and, often, whole washes of light.

"Jon has an unusual energy," says his assistant and partner of eighteen years, Martha McGuire, "and all of his images are suffused with that intensity. He can meditate on a single scene, single-mindedly, and ultimately draw out the hidden essence of that image."

◆ ◆ ◆

But back to Manhattan.

When I first looked at Jon's light-tinctured portraits of the city, I had to shake my head in wonder. Not only was I seeing places I'd never been to personally in my almost two decades as a New Yorker, but when I did recognize a location, it invariably included scenic nuances that had previously—and completely—escaped my glance.

Take, for instance, Central Park. In this book, Jon quietly slips into the Secret Garden, a pastoral reading area within the Park's restored Conservancy Garden, and zooms in on the statue of a water nymph holding a platter at the center of a concrete, lily-padded fountain. In two jarringly intimate photos, Ortner reveals the synchronous sensuality and child-like playfulness of that bronze figurine. I had never seen that statue before (indeed, it is often upstaged by Walter Schott's more popular dancing girls in the Untermeyer Fountain, also photographed for this book); and yet there she was on the page, introducing herself to me, bathed in the breaking glimmer that has become an Ortner trademark.

But even when I happen upon an Ortner image whose location I've actually been to myself—such as his magnificent, sleepy snow-covered bridge photo, also shot in Central Park—two things suddenly become obvious: that Ortner clearly enjoys some sort of conspiratorial relationship with the elements—the light and wind and weather—in a way that makes his pictures unrivaled; and that he'll stop at nothing to unlock the visual mysteries *beneath* each new photograph. He is not satisfied, say those who know him, if his aren't the first footsteps in a new snow in Central Park; and the bridge portrait in this book explains that obsession not only in its unmistakably pristine hues, but in an underlying subtext that suggests the sacredness with which Ortner approached that very bridge, that very snowy day.

But it is in depicting the drama of Manhattan's more sensational structures—its bridges and skyscrapers and landmarks—that Ortner finds his truest calling. In the vibrant travelogue that is *Manhattan Dawn and Dusk*, you will see the Empire State Building captured in diverse incarnations: shrouded in the dawn fog against a gray-purple sky, evincing an almost dangerous, steely severity; or color-lit at dusk, looking for all the world like an enormous candy stick rising into a fantasy land heaven.

You will see the Chrysler Building, once the Empire State's heaven-reaching rival, in close-ups so intimate, so stark, it appears less like a skyscraper than a futuristic beehive of steel. William Van Alen's architectural masterpiece—with its triangular windows and concentric arches regenerating themselves atop one another—has defied duplication by any architect or artist since its construction in 1930; and Ortner's meticulous rendering of it showcases that singularity with practiced perfection.

You will see the Statue of Liberty, New York Harbor's grand dame, in her many vibrant moods: proudly illuminated like a roman candle, burning a hole in the dusk-dampened harbor sky; placid and reverent, in a tight, low-angle shot that includes all three of the statue's most celebrated elements—her crown, her tablet and her torch; or magically appearing on what seems to be the same plot of soil as the World

Trade Towers, as shot by Ortner with a telephoto lens from Caven Point, an abandoned railroad pier.

You will see Rockefeller Center—which Ortner calls "the most beautifully executed piece of New York"—in a nine-page portfolio that serves as much a showcase for the photographer's boundless curiosity as it does an expose of the twenty-two-acre common's infinite charms: the multicolored geometry of the army of world flags that surround the sunken plaza; the angular art deco sentinels—representing *Light* and *Sound*—that hover above the entrance to the seventy-story GE Building; the famed golden statue of Prometheus, appearing almost liquid in its Ortner interpretation, swimming above the Zodiac ring and backed by an awesome sea of Christmas lights; and, in a singular achievement that seems to epitomize Ortner's mastery over his medium, a photograph that features the green-yellow spires of St. Patrick's cathedral at dusk, framed by the sobering towers of Rockefeller Center and fronted by the burnished black statue of Atlas holding the world on his back. In one perfect image, Ortner manages to capture—simultaneously—the theology, mythology and technology that define Manhattan.

You will see Ortner's enchanting rendition of the city's Upper West Side, where the Queen Anne and neo-Renaissance influence often make the buildings appear more like antique wooden puzzles than apartment houses; where the baroque detailing of porticos and turrets and façades lend a homey gingerbread feel to whole city blocks. In stark contrast to this is the genteel austerity of the Upper East Side, where grasses are lawns and lawns are gardens. Here Ortner triumphs again, calling upon the morning light to help him accentuate the sophisticated elegance of this, the most exclusive section of the city. He does this most deftly in a simple, single shot of a pink-blossomed tree blooming outside a Fifth Avenue residence. The effect is at once graceful and breath-taking.

And then, of course, there is the magic of Ortner *discoveries*, a potpourri of small but significant hidden treats, often overlooked by the average on-the-run New Yorker yet never missed by Ortner's roving eye: the colorful chorus line of painted steel jockeys in modest attendance behind the cast iron fence of the 21 Club; the mighty swirl of Frank Lloyd Wright's spiral exterior for the Guggenheim Museum of Art—a design which Ortner explains as an "organic sweep" intended to stand out in a city too often besieged by architectural sameness; a montage of terra cotta faces, stone visages that peer from above the doorways of the city's many brownstones; the simple scarlet perfection of the Naguchi cube (located on the dedication page), counterpointed by the dark façade of a bank peeking through its center; the golden, dawn-soaked walls of the Gothic revival Trinity Church (the oldest in Manhattan), its jewel-box windows so vivid you can almost hear the clink of stained glass; the watchful statue of Hercules, urgent yet gentle, his eye trained on the thirteen-foot clock that stands at the south end of Grand Central Station.

And, oh, those bridges—Brooklyn, Verrazano Narrows, George Washington, Manhattan—their majestic arcs and sweeps caught by Ortner in feats equal parts photographic and mountaineering.

Like most New Yorkers, I feel a simultaneous affinity for, and alienation from, this, the greatest city in the world: its sheer magnitude and vitality can often be so overwhelming as to bedevil even as it bewitches. So I feel especially fortunate to have been treated to Jon's vision of Manhattan, one which gives those two memorable dawn and dusk moments of mine—the ones from the fashion district and Hoboken—a little more texture, a little more perspective, a little more *light*.

◆ ◆ ◆

And, of course, light is what Jon Ortner is all about.

"With just the right light," he says, "and at just the right moment, even a fire escape can become a miraculous thing of beauty. On the other hand," he adds with a smile, "there's actually nothing magical about dawn and dusk, is there? When you get down to it, it's really just one more revolution of the earth."

BRUCE KLUGER

Bruce Kluger is a writer, television personality and an editor at Playboy Magazine. *His work has also appeared in* Glamour, TV Guide *and* Bride's Magazine.

NEW YORK HARBOR

PAGES 16–21:

VERRAZANO NARROWS BRIDGE

IN 1524, THE ITALIAN EXPLORER, Geovanni Verrazano sailed his caravel, "The Dauphine," into the opening of the majestic bay where the East and Hudson rivers empty into the Atlantic. Dropping anchor, he rowed through the lower bay and between the narrows, and for the first time, saw New York Harbor and the island which would later be named Manhattan.

The 690-foot west tower of the Verrazano Narrows Bridge, the largest single span in the world.

Providing access to the top of the Verrazano Narrows Bridge is a tiny elevator which threads its way up the east tower. The final pitch is scaled by climbing an internal rung ladder from which you emerge onto a small platform.

This was my first experience photographing from such an exposed and treacherous vantage, and to stand at the pinnacle of the east tower is to also brave the wind and cold. Not surprisingly, my heart began beating rapidly and I felt breathless. After checking that the camera was securely tied to my wrist, I leaned over the steel ledge to record the bridge's 4,260-foot span and its surrounding landscape of turbulent silver water. The reward was a magnificent 360° view of New York Harbor and the great Atlantic.

Since then, I've climbed the major bridges of New York City several times, controlling the fear yet never losing it completely.

PAGES 22–23:
THE LIBERTY CENTENNIAL

The Statue of Liberty Centennial celebration featured one of the most spectacular firework displays ever created. At a cost of two million dollars, it took the cooperation of six American firework companies. Forty tons of pyrotechnics including 40,000 projectiles were detonated, filling the sky with a dazzling color and light show. Here, the three largest "chrysanthemums" ever launched explode over New York Harbor.

STATUE OF LIBERTY

IMMENSE, YET WITH ELEGANT PROPORTIONS, the Statue of Liberty came from Bartholdi's final 1875 clay-model design entitled "Liberty Enlightening the World." A giantess, Liberty stands 1,250 feet tall and weighs 250 tons. Her 35-foot waist, three-foot wide mouth, and eight-foot long index finger, gives one an idea of her incredible size.

Much of Liberty's beauty comes from more than 100 years of weathering which has caused a rich turquoise patina to form over her thin copper skin. The statue's appearance is ever-changing between sunrise and sunset as her blue-green hue transmutes into an almost endless variety of shades. However, the surface of Liberty is delicate and cannot be cleaned for fear of damaging this layer of protective corrosion.

The land beneath Liberty's feet was originally known as "Bedlow's Island," and although the statue is located within New Jersey's coastal territory, she belongs to New York. A result of one of the oddest property divisions ever drawn up, anything below water in this area belongs to New Jersey, and anything above belongs to New York.

In 1986, the statue underwent a 66 million dollar renovation. Her interior metal armature was bolstered, her crown repaired, and her torch replaced. Small retouches were made on her surface by a skilled French patinist.

LEFT:
The beauty of the Statue of Liberty and its surrounding harbor attract a variety of pleasure craft, including sailboats, yachts, and ocean liners.

RIGHT:
Liberty holds high the Torch of Enlightenment and carries the Book of Law inscribed with the date of the Declaration of Independence. The seven rays of her crown correspond to the seven seas and seven continents of the world.

OPPOSITE:
This unique perspective of the Statue of Liberty can be seen only from Caven Point, a crumbling abandoned pier in New Jersey.

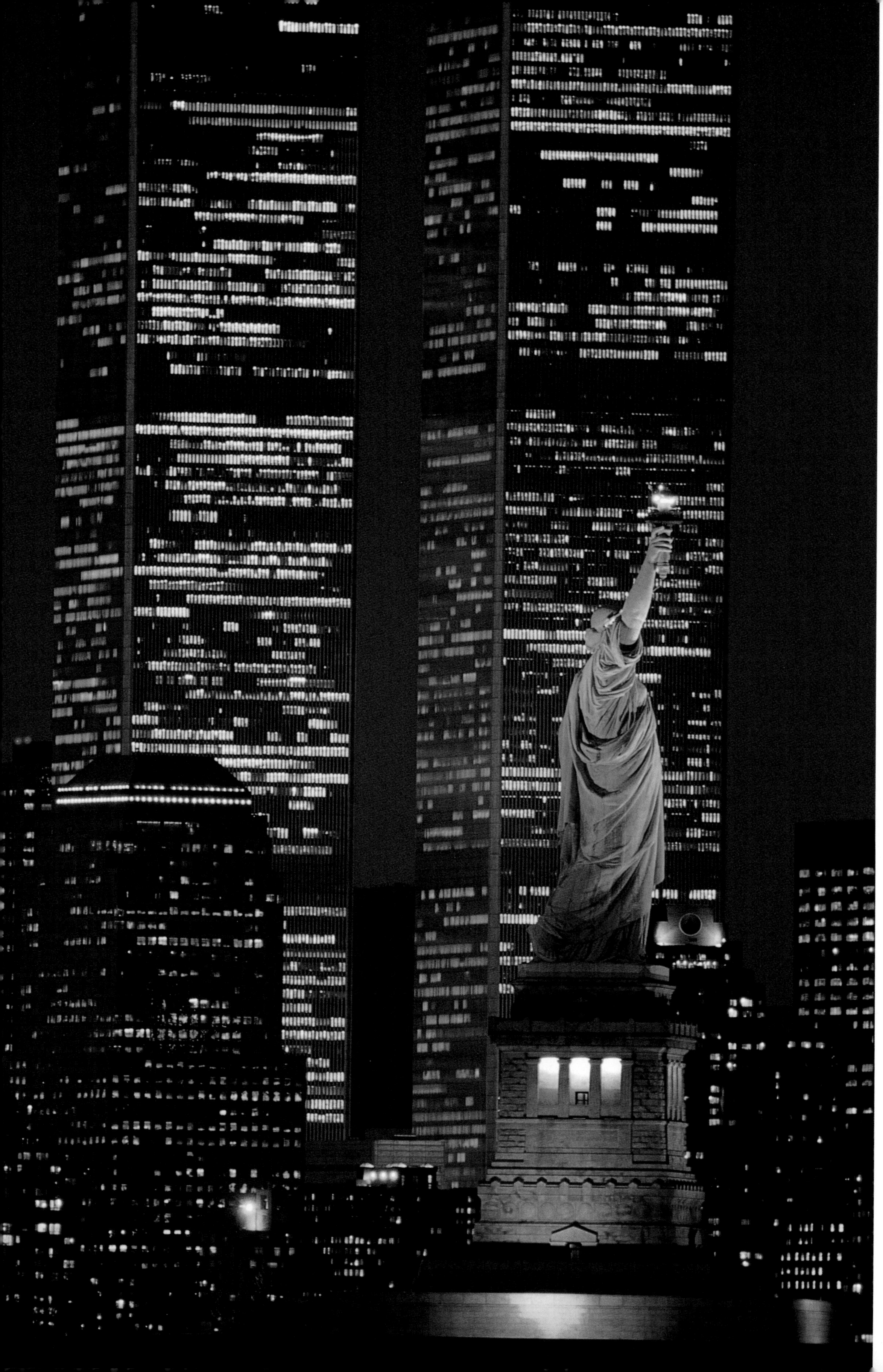

FINANCIAL DISTRICT

Built in 1846, the Trinity Church is the most famous church in New York and the third incarnation erected on the original 1705 land grant site. The flying buttresses and stained glass designed by Richard Upjohn are medievally inspired and typical of Gothic revival architecture.

PAGE 34:
The sun rises between the monolithic Trade
Towers only twice a year.

PAGES 35–38:
WORLD TRADE TOWERS

Art deco figures symbolizing civic responsibility stand guard in front of the 1955 Charles B. Meyers' Department of Health Building at 125 Worth Street.

OPPOSITE:
Daniel Chester French's sculpture occupies the front of the 1907 U.S. Customs House at Bowling Green.

PAGE 39:

An 80-foot pool reflects the light from the glass dome of the World Financial Center's Wintergarden.

Facing the Hudson River is Cesar Pelli's 1988 vaulted glass Wintergarden. The 18,000-square-foot courtyard boasts a grove of 45-foot Washingtonia palms and is ringed by shops and restaurants.

The Three Red Wings, a vermilion-hued, 25-foot Calder stabile located at the base of the Trade Towers, is spotlighted by the rising sun for only a brief ten minutes each morning.

PAGES 42–43:

The New York Stock Exchange, the largest securities exchange in the world, has come a long way from its humble beginnings in 1792 when traders met under a buttonwood tree. The trading floor, two-thirds the size of a football field, is a beehive of activity indecipherable to the uninitiated. Yet what may appear as a frenzy of "buy and sell" is in fact a highly organized system of handling the needs of 30 million shareholders worldwide.

Melvyn Kaufman developed 127 John Street in 1969 to contrast with highbrow
Wall Street architecture. This futuristic pedestrian tunnel and giant digital clock
on the building's exterior are examples of the whimsical design elements
Kaufman employed.

THE VILLAGE

This monumental interpretation of Georges Seurat's pointillistic masterpiece,
La Grande Jatte, is painted upon raw brick walls.

Soho is packed with so many artists that creativity often overflows onto sidewalks and walls, where politics and art merge into expressions of outrage and humor.

PAGES 50–51:
Multicolored fire escapes exemplify the rich history and spectrum of architectural

Once the busiest seaport in America, South Street Seaport fell into decline with
the advent of the steamship. Today, restoration of historic buildings and ships,
which began in the 1960s, continues to revitalize the waterfront.

Classic skyscrapers in their day, the Corinthian colonnades of the Municipal
Building and the neo-Gothic façade of the Woolworth Building are dwarfed by
the minimalist 110-story World Trade Towers.

PAGES 55–62:

BROOKLYN BRIDGE

IN THE WINTER OF 1852, HEAVY ICE FLOES INTERRUPTED FERRY SERVICE across the
East River, inspiring German immigrant John Roebling to conceive the Brooklyn
Bridge. It was intended to be as much a national monument as a connection
between Brooklyn and Manhattan. At the time of its construction, completed in
1883, it was the world's longest suspension bridge and the first to be built of steel.

PAGES 56–57:
View from the Manhattan Bridge.

RIGHT:
Fourteen thousand miles of steel wire are woven into the cables of the incredibly stable Brooklyn Bridge.

PAGES 60–61:
These Gothic-style granite towers, or caissons, took five years to complete and were sunk nearly 100 feet below the river bed.

The Brooklyn Bridge's Centennial was marked by a full moon and a celebration of fireworks by Grucci Brothers. A crew of 22 men worked three days to set up a show using 9,000 shells fired from nine barges and three tugs. A pyrotechnic "Niagara Falls" of fire cascaded from the bottom of the bridge into the East River.

MANHATTAN BRIDGE

The East River has always seemed windier than the Hudson, and the evening of my climb was no different. As I ascended the long main cable of the Manhattan Bridge, I was buffeted by the high winds funnelling down the channel. Each time a subway clattered by, the bridge would heave and shake.

As I neared the east tower, the cable became very steep, requiring an awkward maneuver to step onto its ornate metal deck. But once there, I was greeted by an unparalleled panoramic view and necklaces of steel and lights sweeping down to meet the city.

In 1903, Manhattan Bridge was an engineering innovation, designed to hold heavier loads than its predecessors. Today, its 1,470-foot span and exposed-steel trussing can support cars on the upper level and subways on the lower.

RIGHT:
Brooklyn from the east tower of
the Manhattan Bridge.

PAGES 68–69:
In 1611, after hearing Henry
Hudson's report to the Dutch
East India Company, Dutch
adventurer and trader Adrian
Block was the first to sail his
yacht up the surging tides of the
East River. Both the Manhattan
Bridge and the Brooklyn Bridge
can be seen in this more recent
view.

Tucked away on a Greenwich Village side street, a floral ceramic panel has sur-
vived since 1868.

OPPOSITE:
In the 1840s, a potter's field and hanging gallows was transformed into
Washington Square Park. Surrounding the park, this row of Greek revival houses,
fronted in red brick, white marble steps, and guarded by this stone lion, was built
for the prominent banking and merchant families of the era.

MIDTOWN

Shown here in holiday attire is one of Edward C. Potter's two majestic marble lions at the entrance to the New York Public Library. Designed by Thomas Hastings in 1911, the building is one of the finest beaux-arts structures in America.

OPPOSITE:

The Flatiron Building owes its unique triangular shape to the plot on which it was built. At the turn of the century, the building was made famous by the photographs of Alfred Steiglitz and Edward Steichen, and even today is a well known symbol of New York City.

This awe-inspiring view from the top of the Empire State Building stretches from the Hudson to the East rivers. Midtown office buildings dominate to the north and the George Washington Bridge can be seen on the far left horizon.

JACOB JAVIT*S* CONVENTION CENTER

Designed in 1987 by James Freed of I. M. Pei and Partners, the Jacob Javits Convention Center is one of the world's largest buildings, encompassing 1.8 million square feet. The center's transparent exterior is constructed of more than 16,000 glass panels that provide 100,000 square feet of skylight.

OPPOSITE:
Giant structural pillars called "champagne columns" support the roof of the 150-foot piazza.

The 1926 clock tower of the ConEd Building was designed by Warren & Wetmore, the same architects who designed Grand Central Terminal.

PAGES 81–86:

EMPIRE *STATE* BUILDING

On a clear day, visibility from the top of the Empire State Building extends up to 80 miles. But like a mountain peak, this 60,000-ton building causes huge updrafts and anomalous weather conditions such as rain and snow that appear to fall upward.

RIGHT AND PAGE 84:
Red and green are only two of the ever-changing colors the Empire State Building displays to correspond with special events and holidays. While the mast panel's lights are remotely controlled, the huge floodlights set at four corners of the lower stories require six hours for an electrical crew to change.

In 1930, fierce competition arose to erect the world's tallest structure. In a surprise last minute move, a 123-foot stainless steel spire was added to the Chrysler Building, making it surpass all others. The victory was short-lived, as the Empire State Building stole the title just a few months later.

CHRYSLER BUILDING

DESIGNED BY WILLIAM
VAN ALEN as Walter
Chrysler's monument to the
automobile, the Chrysler
Building's embellishments
include eagle gargoyles
resembling hood ornaments,
and chrome-studded hub-
caps set into a brickwork
frieze of stylized racing
cars.

LEFT AND OPPOSITE:
Concentric arches of exposed
stainless steel accentuate the
Chrysler Building's unconven-
tional triangular windows. In
1981, according to Van Alen's
original design, spectacular lighting was installed, giving this
landmark structure one of the
most distinctive profiles in the
nocturnal New York skyline.

Midtown skyline, as seen from atop the New Jersey Palisades at the site of the 1804 Hamilton and Burr duel.

Just as a New York egg cream does not contain eggs, Times Square is actually a triangle. Located at the convergence of Seventh Avenue and Broadway, it is considered the heart of the theater district. Once called Longacre Square, it was renamed when *The New York Times* moved to 43rd Street.

An art deco masterpiece, Radio City Music Hall is America's largest indoor
theater. Each year, over five million people come to its musicals, concerts, and
special film screenings.

GRAND CENTRAL TERMINAL

The 375-foot main concourse of Grand Central Terminal is one of the most impressive halls in Manhattan. Built by Cornelius Vanderbilt in 1871 as a rail palace and gateway to the city, its 125-foot-high vaulted ceiling features ornately painted constellations and lighted stars.

Hercules frames the 13-foot clock that crowns the southern entrance to Grand
Central Terminal.

TOP:
The Helmsley Building clock has overlooked Park Avenue since 1929.

ROCKEFELLER CENTER

PAGES 98–99:

Paul Manship's 1934 gilded bronze figure of Prometheus, set above an engraved gold Zodiac ring, dominates Rockefeller Center and appears to be floating on air. Fifty electronically-controlled water jets and computerized colored lights bathe the Greek god who brought fire to man.

BELOW:

Accentuated by a series of architectural setbacks, the 70-story GE Building, formerly the RCA Building, accommodates many prestigious tenants, among them the world-famous supper club The Rainbow Room.

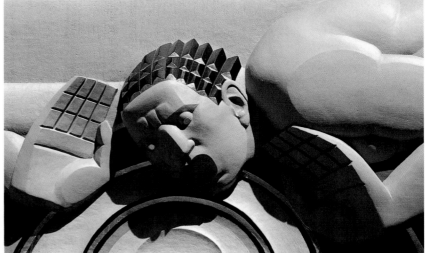

World flags surround the sunken plaza of Rockefeller Center.

TOP:

Looking down on the entrance to the GE Building are the art deco figures known as *Light* and *Sound*.

OPPOSITE:

The annual lighting of the Christmas tree in Rockefeller Center is a very popular event and marks the beginning of the busy holiday season. Each year the tree is carefully selected from among the tallest and most perfect evergreens in New England.

A bronze turtle suns himself in the Channel Garden's granite pool. Glass panels set into the bottom turn the water a luminous green.

RIGHT:
Inspired by the English Channel, the 200-foot long Channel Garden separates the French and British buildings of Rockefeller Center. In warm weather, lush displays of flowering shrubs and trees, orchids and topiaries enhance its bronze fountains. The winter season is celebrated by giant twinkling snowflakes and trumpeting angels which lead to the Christmas tree.

PAGE 104:
St. Patrick's Cathedral forms a dramatic backdrop for Lee Laurie's colossal Atlas, designed in 1937.

PAGE 105:
Facing Fifth Avenue, Atlas, standing 15 feet tall and weighing seven tons, triumphantly shoulders the world.

TRUMP TOWER

The reflection of the Crown Building mingles with Christmas trees in the black faceted setbacks of Trump Tower. It is the prestigious address of moguls and stars who reside in its 68 stories of condominiums.

OPPOSITE:
Escalators move discerning customers up through the five-story skylit atrium of Trump Tower. Resplendent in pink marble, mirrored waterfalls, and tropical foliage, the atrium features European specialty shops.

The City Center 55th Street Theater was originally built as a Shriner's temple.
The detail above shows the glazed ceramic pillars of Islamic and Moorish design.

Still standing from Prohibition days, mementos such as horse-and-carriage hitching posts and a jockey hall of fame decorate the entrance to the famous 21 Club. Known then as Jack and Charlie's Place, the restaurant at 21 West 52nd Street was converted from an 1870s brownstone.

The Lipstick Building, as it is informally called, mirrors surrounding skyscrapers, including the Citicorp Building. Streamlined, elliptical contours of tapered glass and pink stone are hallmarks of this unique structure, designed by renowned architects John Burgee and Philip Johnson.

The Lipstick Building, as reflected off the multifaceted exterior of 875 Third Avenue.

In many skyscrapers, glass panes are equipped with sensors that monitor and adjust temperature as well as the amount of sunlight entering the building.

The work of an international committee of architects, the 544-foot glass-covered
slab of the Secretariat Building of the United Nations was completed in 1953.

PAGES 115–118:

EAST SIDE SKYLINE

The Chrysler Building is reflected in the black glass of the Grand Hyatt.

ALL SKYSCRAPERS MUST BE
flexible enough withstand the
stress that winds and even earth-
quakes produce. Though tall
buildings normally experience
many kinds of movement,
among them drift, sway, and
twist, the top of a 1,000-foot
tower should not sway more
than two-and-a-half feet. One
back-and-forth motion, or oscil-
lation, at the World Trade
Towers takes ten seconds; the
more rigid Citicorp's time is
seven seconds. To cope with this
vibration, Citicorp installed a
"Tuned Mass Damper," a 400-
ton block attached to a massive
spring nestled deep in the heart
of the building. A gargantuan
shock absorber, it is tuned to
vibrate at the same rate as the
45-story building.

Today's skyscraper architects have a tremendous variety of reflective materials with which to work, often transforming windows and mirrors into urban kaleidoscopes.

The gilded equestrian statue of General William Tecumseh Sherman being led by the angel Winged Victory stands opposite the Pulitzer Fountain.

RIGHT:
Sparkling in holiday adornment are Fifth Avenue and the Pulitzer Fountain topped by Pomona, the Roman goddess of abundance.

QUEENSBORO BRIDGE

COMMONLY KNOWN AS THE 59TH STREET
BRIDGE, the cantilevered Queensboro Bridge connects midtown Manhattan with Long Island.
Because of financial and political delays, forty
years elapsed between the time of its design and
completion. Almost 50,000 tons of steel were
used to create a complex lattice topped by finials
resembling a queen chess piece.

CENTRAL PARK

SPRING

By the mid 1800s, unbridled growth of stone and concrete threatened to smother the entire surface of Manhattan. In 1856, the city bought most of the land which became Central Park for five million dollars. Four to five million trees of 632 species were planted and an additional 800 species of vines and bushes were also integrated into the landscape. Ten million cartloads of dirt were shifted to meet the elegant design demands of Vaux and Olmsted. Slowly and subtly, over the course of 20 years, these 840 acres began to take on an aura combining the formality of European gardens with a sense of the English countryside. Today, many New Yorkers could not envision living in this city without their Central Park "oasis."

The 1885 *Pilgrim Memorial* was created by John Quincy Adams Ward.

OPPOSITE:
The 224-ton obelisk Cleopatra's Needle is certainly the most venerable piece of public sculpture in the city. Erected sometime around 1500 B.C. by Thutmose III, it stood in Heliopolis for a thousand years before it was moved by the Romans to stand near a temple to Cleopatra. Given to New York City by the Khedive of Egypt, it was installed in 1881. Sadly, more damage has been done to it by New York's corrosive atmosphere in one century than in the 3,000 years it stood in the desert.

SUMMER

The Secret Garden, named after Frances Hodgson Burnett's classic children's story, is an area designed for reading and meditation. This tranquil sancturary is located within the Conservatory Garden, a site restored and maintained by the Central Park Conservancy.

The centerpiece of the Conservatory Garden is the Untermeyer Fountain, higlighted by Walter Schott's 1947 lifesize bronze depicting girls dancing with joyous abandon. The fountain is surrounded by formal plantings and circular beds which blossom with seasonal displays.

The 1871 Belevedere Castle seems to grow from its foundation of bedrock. Named Vista Rock, this 140-foot outcrop is the highest point in Central Park and one of its few pieces of original topography.

AUTUMN

Angel of the Waters, a bronze by Emma Stebbins, stands in the center of the elaborate brick terrace at the heart of Central Park. Symbolizing the angel who conferred healing powers upon the Bethesda Pool in Jerusalem, she is held aloft by the four cherubs Temperance, Purity, Health, and Peace. Once used for watering horses, the fountain is now a meeting place for dogwalkers and rollerbladers.

The 1859 cast-iron Bow Bridge crosses the Lake and leads to the Ramble.

WINTER

Perhaps no other place in New York City has the serenity, beauty, and solitude of
Central Park after a dense snowstorm. Many things people associate with the city
are strangely, almost eerily missing—crowds, noise, dirt—purified and silenced
by a deep, soft blanket of white.

Driven by my passion for the ultimate images of New York City, I have always tried to be the first person in Central Park after a winter storm. It was never easy. Within moments of sunrise, the pristine snowscape would succumb to joggers, dogwalkers, and cross-country skiers. Over the years I would arrive earlier and earlier, sometimes leaving my apartment at four A.M. Several rare and wonderful mornings I hiked the stony outcrops and frozen glens, finding myself completely alone and photographing vistas without a single errant footprint.

Snowfall plays an important role in the search for the perfect landscape; the bigger the storm, the deeper the drifts. Paths become tunnels, and familiar scenery looks fresh, making the park seem a place of secret wilderness and adventure.

The triple-towered Beresford on Central Park West is viewed from the wooden gazebo atop Vista Rock.

LEFT:

A dense blanket of snow covers the miniature Gothic Belevedere Castle as if in a fairy tale.

The stone Gapstow Bridge crosses the north inlet of the Pond. In a background
of mist appear the ghostly outlines of the Plaza Hotel and other high-rises south
of Central Park.

After a winter snow, the glass-enclosed Tavern on the Green is aglow. Built in 1934 on the site of a former sheepfold, the restaurant has since charmed generations of diners with its opulent decor and lovely views of Central Park.

UPPER WEST SIDE

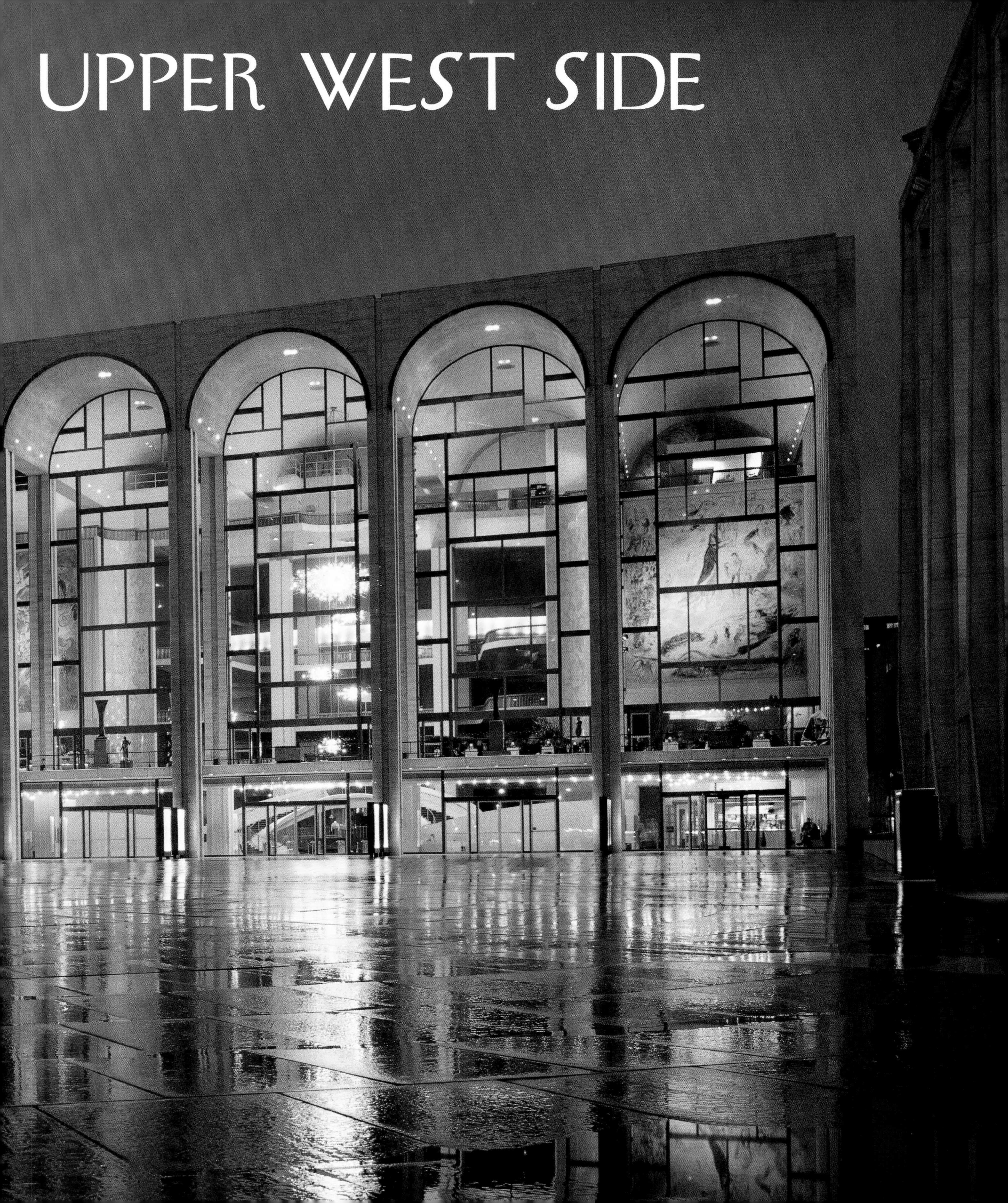

PAGES 156–157:
Each year more than 3,000 performances, from free outdoor band concerts to extravagant operas, are held at Lincoln Center—the preeminent cultural and performing arts center of the world. Here, the classical arches of the Metropolitan Opera House are mirrored in the rain-washed travertine of the central plaza, adding to the elegance imparted by Chagall's murals and the fountain designed by Philip Johnson.

Framed by Ionic columns, the 1939 equestrian statue of Theodore Roosevelt, accompanied by an Indian chief and a Bantu warrior, greets visitors at the Central Park West entrance to the Museum of Natural History, the world's largest museum. Begun in 1869, during the "golden era of natural history," this 1.5 million-square-foot Gothic castle of pink granite houses more than 36 million specimens.

The Central Park West Historic District stretches south along West 90th to West 62nd streets. Development, which began in the late 1800s, resulted in a mosaic of distinctive buildings constructed in neo-Renaissance, Queen Anne, and Romanesque revival styles. The neighborhood declined during the Great Depression of 1929, but in the 1960s, the newly-built Lincoln Center attracted performers, artists, and the affluent who gentrified and restored the area.

The rich color and baroque detail of the 1889 Evelyn Building on West 79th Street was achieved using unglazed terra cotta and brick.

These Romanesque- and Queen Anne-style buildings are trimmed with wrought-iron, stained glass, and copper.

Thomas Lamb, known for his extravagant movie palaces, designed the Pythian
Temple which was built in 1927 as a Masonic Grand Lodge. The use of sphinx,
vulture, and pharoah images on the temple's polychromate panels reflects an
interest in Egyptology, fostered by the discovery of Tutankhamen's tomb in 1922.

Moorish- and Roman-style details decorate the columns of Congregation B'nai Jeshurun, New York's oldest Ashkenazic synagogue.

This wrought-iron gate can be found on West End Avenue.

When first built in 1884, the Dakota apartment building was ridiculed for being so far uptown that "it might as well be in the Dakotas." But it turned out to be ahead of its time, quickly becoming the most prestigious address of the Upper West Side and the residence of such notables as Lauren Bacall, Leonard Bernstein, Boris Karloff, and John Lennon. This detail of the original cast-iron fence was forged in Brooklyn by Hecla Iron Works.

UPPER EAST SIDE

PAGES 174–175:
The distinctive spiral of the Solomon R. Guggenheim Museum was described as "organic architecture" by its creator Frank Lloyd Wright. Reflecting his love of natural shapes, the reverse spiral is reminiscent of a chambered nautilus shell. Lit by a circular skylight, the quarter mile ramp inside the museum takes visitors through one of the finest collections of abstract art in the world.

The Metropolitan Museum of Art, the largest art museum in the world, is also New York City's most popular tourist attraction and defines the city's status as a cultural epicenter. The beaux-arts central façade was designed by Richard Morris Hunt in 1902 as a palace worthy of imperial Rome and the dramatic main entrance comprises monumental triple arches framed by four pairs of Corinthian columns.

An elegant copper and glass canopy, circa 1903, covers the entrance to the famous home of steel magnate Andrew Carnegie. Known today as the Cooper Hewitt Museum, it houses the Smithsonian's National Institute of Design.

OPPOSITE:
This serene formal garden, designed by Russell Page, was added to the Frick Museum in 1977. The Ionic columns and floor-to-ceiling arched windows are faithful to the 18th century French style incorporated by Carrère and Hastings.

Spring arrives at the doorstep of elegant residences on Fifth Avenue, the home of more museums than any other street in the city. The area between 79th and 106th streets is nicknamed "Museum Mile" and includes among others, the Metro-politan Museum of Art, the Frick, the Cooper Hewitt, the International Center of Photography, and the Guggenheim.

OPPOSITE:
A stone dragon sits in front of a historic townhouse on 78th Street off Fifth Avenue.

The banded arches and Saracenic detail of the 1890 Park East Synagogue represent ties to the 19th century Jewish culture of Moorish Spain.

OPPOSITE:
The French neo-Gothic arches of the belfry soar above the Episcopal Church of Holy Trinity on East 88th Street. J. Stewart Barney created this 1897 Victorian masterpiece out of golden-brown brick and terra cotta.

The granite exterior and spare geometric design of the 1991 Islamic Culture Center is the work of Skidmore, Owings, and Merrill. Its copper dome and minaret were designed by Swanke, Hayden, and Connell. In order to face Mecca, the building is angled 29° off the perpendicular intersection at 96th Street and Third Avenue.

The baroque St. Nicholas Cathedral, tucked away on 97th Street is the diocesan seat of the Russian Orthodox Church in America. Ornamented with carved cherubs, golden crosses, and blue and yellow tiles, the graystone structure is capped by five onion-domed cupolas.

Designed by Napoleon LeBrun, St. Cecelia Roman Catholic Church was completed in 1887. The skillfully constructed façade features a one-and-a-half-story bas-relief of St. Cecilia playing the organ.

Traffic courses up and down the wide expanse of Park Avenue, which is flanked by mirrored office buildings and the golden Helmsley to the south, and prestigious residences further north.

This townhouse in the French classical style is located in the Metropolitan Museum Historical District.

Deco nudes, designed by Wheeler Williams in 1950, recline above the entrance to
Sotheby Realty on Madison Avneue.

PAGES 192–193:
A landscaped island divides the four generous lanes of traffic on Park Avenue.
The meticulously maintained trees and flowers are sponsored by local residents.

NORTHERN

MANHATTAN

At the center of the cruciform floor plan of St. Paul's Chapel at Columbia
University is a 48-foot dome decorated with Guastavino tile in a Byzantine motif.

Though Riverside Church is a modern steel-supported structure, it owes its Gothic inspiration to Chartres Cathedral. The interdenominational church holds 2,500 worshippers. The chancel, shown here, is graced with carved images of the prophets and an elaborate screen illustrating Christ's Divine Ideals.

True to its name, the Triborough Bridge connects the three boroughs of Manhattan, the Bronx, and Queens and was opened in 1936 after two years of debate and planning. The suspension bridge spans 1,380 feet and runs from Randall's Island across the East River to Long Island. Its 10,800 miles of steel wires support eight lanes of traffic as well as pedestrian walkways.

GEORGE WASHINGTON BRIDGE

Completed by engineer Othmar H. Ammann in 1931, the George Washington Bridge was the most daring project of its day. It spans 3,500 feet across the Hudson River, doubling the record for suspension bridges. The 604-foot raw steel towers contain 17-story arches through which 50 million cars pass annually from New Jersey to Manhattan. Four cables containing 105,000 miles of wire, curve gracefully from the towers, prompting Le Corbusier to call the George Washington Bridge "the only seat of grace in this disordered city."

THE CLOISTERS

Several monastic cloisters and Gothic chapels, dating from the 12th to 13th centuries, were shipped from France and Spain and reassembled on a magnificent site overlooking the Hudson River.

OPPOSITE:

The Cloisters house the Metropolitan Museum's collection of medieval art, including the Unicorn Tapestries and sculpture gathered by George Gray Barnard.

The 2,900-foot span of the Throgs Neck Bridge arches over the Whitestone and Queensboro bridges and a distant New York skyline.

Published in 1995 and distributed in the U.S. by
Stewart, Tabori & Chang,
a division of U.S. Media Holdings, Inc.
115 West 18th Street, New York, NY 10011

Distributed in Canada by General Publishing Co. Ltd., 30 Lesmill Road, Don Mills, Ontario, Canada M3B 2T6. Distributed in the U.K. by Hi Marketing, 38 Carver Road, London, SE24 9LT, England. Distibuted in Europe by Onslow Books Ltd., Tyler's Court, 111A Wardour Street, London, W1V 3TD, England. Sold in Australia by Peribo Pty Limited, 58 Beaumont Road, Mount Kuring-gai, NSW, 2080, Australia.

DESIGNED BY
Nai Y. Chang

EDITED BY
Mary Kalamaras

PRODUCTION BY
Alice Wong

Library of Congress Cataloging-in-Publication Data

Ortner, Jon. 1951–
Manhattan dawn and dusk / Jon Ortner.
    p.   cm.
    ISBN 1-55670-426-7
    I. Manhattan (New York, N.Y.)—Pictorial works. 2. New York (N.Y.)—
Pictorial works. I. Title.
F128.37.O78 1995   95–22256
974.7'1—dc20   CIP

Printed in Japan
10 9 8 7 6 5 4 3 2